# S U S H I

MARKS &
SPENCER

# SUSHI

## LULU GRIMES

Marks and Spencer p.l.c.
Baker Street, London, W1U 8EP

T21/7688/5306A

www.marksandspencer.com

ISBN: 1-84461-025-X

Printed in China

Produced by the Bridgewater Book Company Ltd

Photographer: David Jordan

Home Economist: Jacqueline Bellefontaine

Notes for the Reader

This book uses both metric and imperial measurements. Follow the same units of measurement throughout; do not mix metric and imperial. All spoon measurements are level: teaspoons are assumed to be 5 ml, and tablespoons are assumed to be 15 ml. Unless otherwise stated, milk is assumed to be full fat, eggs and individual vegetables such as potatoes are medium and pepper is freshly ground black pepper. Recipes using raw or very lightly cooked eggs should be avoided by infants, the elderly, pregnant women, convalescents and anyone suffering from an illness. The times given are an approximate guide only. Preparation times differ according to the techniques used by different people and the cooking times may also vary from those given. Optional ingredients, variations or serving suggestions have not been included in the calculations.

**Picture acknowledgments**
The Bridgewater Book Company would like to thank Corbis Images for permission to reproduce copyright material on pages 1, 7, 8, 30, 52, 74

# CONTENTS

# RAW FISH FOR SUSHI

Sushi is traditionally made using both raw and cooked fish. If you would like to make sushi with raw fish you must realize that this will add an element of risk to your eating experience. Raw fish is more likely to contain bacteria and parasites than cooked fish because it has not been subjected to the required amount of heat to kill them off. Freezing and then thawing raw fish may eliminate some problems but it will not make the fish completely safe, nor will it benefit the texture and flavour. All of the sushi recipes in this book can be made with cooked fish. If you prefer to use raw fish, then you should follow the guidelines below.

People with certain diseases (such as diabetes or liver disease) or weakened immune systems should never eat raw fish or shellfish. Levels of mercury, which is found in water from naturally occurring sources as well as industrial pollution, tend to be higher in long-lived, larger fish with darker meat, such as swordfish, king mackerel and tuna. The elderly and pregnant women (along with nursing mothers and young children) should avoid eating these types of fish.

## BUYING RAW FISH

You must be particularly careful when buying raw fish, it needs to be as fresh as possible and come from a reputable supplier. Fish should only be bought from a supplier or shop that sells 'sushi grade' or 'sashimi grade' fish. This fish is often pre-cut into blocks so that all you have to do is slice it into the required sizes. Buy shellfish that has come from certified waters. Once you have bought your fish you will need to take it straight home in a cold bag with some ice (usually available from the supplier) and put it in the fridge immediately. Use it on the day that you buy it.

## PREPARING RAW FISH

Once you start your recipe, prepare everything else BEFORE you take the fish out of the fridge, then use it quickly, and put the finished sushi back in the fridge as soon as it is made. Keep everything scrupulously clean. Take your sushi out of the fridge just before serving and don't leave it to sit out for any length of time. Hand plates around rather than putting them out for people to help themselves. Ideally, make the sushi at the last minute and serve it straight away.

How to tell if fish and shellfish is fresh (applicable to both raw and cooked):

- Look for firm flesh that bounces back when pressed.
- Fish eyes should be clear and shiny.
- Gills should be bright pink or red with no slime.
- The fish should smell like the ocean not 'fishy'.
- Scales should be shiny and cling tightly to the skin.
- Shells of live clams, mussels and oysters may be open but will close tightly when tapped.
- Live crabs and lobster will be moving.
- Prawns will smell fresh.

How to tell if fish and shellfish is properly cooked:

- When cooked, fish flesh should be opaque and flake easily with a fork.
- Prawns should turn pink and have white, firm flesh.
- Scallops turn an opaque white and firm up.
- Clams, mussels and oysters are done when their shells open; throw away any that stay closed.

## COMMON TYPES OF SUSHI AND SASHIMI GRADE FISH

*maguro,* tuna

*toro,* fatty tuna cut from the belly

*hamachi,* yellowtail

*katsuo,* bonito

*saba,* mackerel

*sake,* salmon

*hirame,* halibut

*suzuki,* sea bass

*unagi,* freshwater eel (this is sold cooked)

*tako,* octopus

*ika,* squid

*awabi,* abalone

*kani,* crab

Sushi is essentially a selection of toppings, traditionally raw fish, pressed onto seasoned rice. But as anyone who loves sushi knows, in practice it is much more than that. It is nice to look at, delicious to eat and pleasurable to make. Modern sushi does not have to be made from raw fish; cooked fish, meats, vegetables and eggs are all used to make a range of colourful, interesting and innovative toppings and fillings. Providing an ingredient will marry well with the flavour of sushi rice, it will make good sushi.

Making sushi requires a little practice; however it is actually much easier than it looks. You don't need lots of equipment, but if you have access to a Japanese shop or a good cook shop then

# INTRODUCTION

you can buy a special bamboo mixing tub *(hangiri or sushi-oke)*, pressing box *(oshi waku)* and rice spatula *(shamoji)*, though none are essential. All you really need is a sushi mat *(makisu)*. The recipes include suggested garnishes, but sushi is wonderful for experimenting with different styles of presentation and decoration.

Rolled sushi, or *maki-zushi*, is a very popular
way of making sushi. Unlike finger sushi, which is
quite hard to make well, rolled sushi needs only
a little practice. A sheet of nori (see page 24) is
spread with rice and fillings and rolled up. The
roll can then be cut into bite-sized pieces, which
are served cut-side up so that you can see the
filling. Sushi rolls can also be served whole if
you prefer. They make a good lunchbox option
for both adults and children if you wrap each
roll in clingfilm.

Rolled sushi is often filled with vegetables or
pickles, pieces of cooked meat, chicken or duck,
cooked fish or seafood. For children's sushi you

# PART ONE
# ROLLING YOUR OWN

can also use sticks of ham or cheese. Sushi rolls
use only a small amount of filling, so you can
choose quite expensive ingredients such as
lobster and crab. You can also choose whether
to make fat or thin rolls.

Once you have made your rolls, you need to
cut them with a very sharp, damp knife to stop
the rice sticking. Traditionally sushi is dipped into
Japanese soy sauce (shoyu), but you can use
mayonnaise or sweet chilli sauce if you like.
Rolled sushi makes a fantastic canapé or starter
for a dinner party. Arrange the pieces of sushi
on a square or rectangular plate and add a small
pile of pickled ginger and wasabi to one corner.

# SUSHI RICE

**ENOUGH FOR 24 PIECES**

250 g/9 oz sushi rice

325 ml/11½ oz water

1 piece of kombu (optional)

2 tbsp sushi rice seasoning

Wash the sushi rice under cold running water until the water running through it is completely clear, then drain the rice. Put the rice in a saucepan with the water and the kombu, if you are using it, cover and bring to the boil as quickly as you can. Remove the kombu, then turn the heat down and simmer for 10 minutes.

Turn off the heat and let the rice stand for 15 minutes. Do not at any point take the lid off the saucepan once you have removed the kombu.

Put the hot rice in a *sushi-oke* (large, very shallow bowl) and pour the sushi rice seasoning evenly over the surface of the rice. Now you will need to use both hands, one to mix the seasoning into the rice with quick cutting strokes using a *shamoji* (spatula) and the other to fan the sushi rice in order to cool it down as quickly as you can. Mix the seasoning in carefully – you do not want to break a single rice grain.

The sushi rice should look shiny and be at room temperature when you are ready to use it.

RICE IS THE MOST IMPORTANT INGREDIENT IN SUSHI. THERE ARE SEVERAL BRANDS OF SUSHI RICE ON THE MARKET. ALL ARE WHITE AND SHORT-GRAIN, AND MARKED SPECIFICALLY 'SUSHI RICE'. IF YOU CAN'T FIND SUSHI RICE, THEN USE ANOTHER TYPE OF SHORT-GRAINED WHITE RICE.

# CALIFORNIA ROLLS

**MAKES 24 PIECES**

1 quantity freshly cooked sushi rice (see page 10)

6 small sheets of toasted nori

wasabi paste

1/2 ripe avocado, cut into batons

6 crab sticks, split in half lengthways

5-cm/2-inch piece of cucumber, peeled and cut into batons

*To serve*

shoyu (Japanese soy sauce)

pickled ginger

Divide the rice into 6 equal portions. Put a sheet of nori shiny-side down on a rolling mat with the longest end towards you and, using wet hands, spread 1 portion of the rice in an even layer on the nori, leaving 2 cm/3/4 inch of nori visible at the end farthest away from you. Don't squash the rice or make the layer too thick – you should be able to see the nori through the rice.

Spread a small amount of wasabi onto the rice at the end nearest you. Lay 2 avocado batons down on top of the wasabi, keeping them parallel to the edge of the nori nearest you, then put 2 pieces of crab next to them. Add a line of cucumber batons.

To roll the sushi, fold the mat over, starting at the end where the ingredients are and tucking in the end of the nori to start the roll. Keep rolling, lifting up the mat as you go and keeping the pressure even but gentle until you have finished the roll. Moisten the top edge of the nori with water to seal the sushi roll closed. Don't worry if anything falls out of the sides, just push it back in. The edges may well look ragged, but don't worry.

Remove the roll from the mat and cut it into 4 even-sized pieces with a wet, very sharp knife. If you don't use a sharp knife the roll will squash as you cut it. Arrange the rolls on a plate. Repeat with the remaining ingredients. Serve with shoyu, pickled ginger and some extra wasabi paste.

CRAB STICKS, SOMETIMES CALLED IMITATION CRAB STICKS, ARE WIDELY AVAILABLE. MADE FROM FISH OR SEAFOOD, THEY ARE NEATLY SHAPED LOGS WITH A PINK STRIP DOWN ONE SIDE. CRAB STICKS ARE FOUND IN CALIFORNIA ROLLS, BUT BECAUSE OF THEIR NEAT SHAPE THEY ARE ALSO VERY USEFUL FOR OTHER TYPES OF ROLLED SUSHI.

# SALMON, ASPARAGUS & MAYONNAISE ROLLS

**MAKES 24 PIECES**

6 asparagus spears

150-g/5¹/₂-oz piece of salmon fillet or the same amount of sushi-grade salmon, cut into batons

1 tbsp oil

1 quantity freshly cooked sushi rice (see page 10)

6 small sheets of toasted nori

wasabi paste

1 tbsp Japanese mayonnaise

1 tsp toasted sesame seeds

*To serve*

shoyu (Japanese soy sauce)

pickled ginger

Lay the asparagus flat in a frying pan filled with simmering water and cook until tender when pierced with the tip of a knife. Cut into 9-cm/3¹/₂-inch lengths and leave to cool.

If using the salmon fillet, pull the skin off and remove any bones. Heat the oil in a frying pan and cook the salmon over a medium heat on both sides for 8 minutes, or until it is cooked through. Cool and flake into large pieces.

Divide the rice into 6 equal portions. Put a sheet of nori shiny-side down on a rolling mat with the longest end towards you and, using wet hands, spread 1 portion of the rice in an even layer on the nori, leaving 2 cm/³/₄ inch of nori visible at the end farthest away from you.

Spread a small amount of wasabi onto the rice at the end nearest you, then spread on the mayonnaise. Lay an asparagus spear on top of the mayonnaise, then put some of the salmon next to it. Sprinkle the sesame seeds on top.

To roll the sushi, fold the mat over, starting at the end where the ingredients are and tucking in the end of the nori to start the roll. Keep rolling, lifting up the mat as you go and keeping the pressure even but gentle until you have finished the roll. Moisten the top edge of the nori with water to seal the sushi roll closed.

Remove the roll from the mat and cut it into 4 even-sized pieces with a wet, very sharp knife. Turn the pieces on end and arrange them on a plate. Repeat with the remaining ingredients. Serve with shoyu, pickled ginger and some extra wasabi paste.

JAPANESE MAYONNAISE IS ALSO CALLED 'KEWPIE MAYONNAISE' BECAUSE OF THE KEWPIE DOLL LOGO USED BY THE COMPANY. IT USUALLY COMES IN A PLASTIC BOTTLE WITHIN A BAG PRINTED WITH A KEWPIE DOLL OUTLINE. YOU CAN USE ORDINARY MAYONNAISE INSTEAD, THOUGH A WHOLE EGG MAYONNAISE WILL TASTE BETTER AS IT TENDS TO BE LESS VINEGARY OR SWEET.

# CRAB, ASPARAGUS & SHIITAKE ROLLS WITH PONZU SAUCE

**MAKES 24 PIECES**

6 asparagus spears

1 tbsp oil

6 shiitake mushrooms, sliced

1 quantity freshly cooked sushi rice (see page 10)

6 small sheets of toasted nori

wasabi paste

6 crab sticks, split in half lengthways

*Ponzu Sauce*

3 tbsp mirin

2 tbsp rice vinegar

1 tbsp light soy sauce

2 tbsp bonito flakes

4 tbsp lemon juice

Lay the asparagus flat in a frying pan filled with simmering water and cook until tender when pierced with the tip of a knife. Cut into 9-cm/3<sup>1</sup>/2-inch lengths and leave to cool.

Heat the oil in a frying pan and cook the mushrooms over a medium heat for 5 minutes, or until completely soft.

To make the Ponzu Sauce, put all the ingredients in a small saucepan and bring to the boil. Once they have boiled, turn off the heat and cool the sauce.

Divide the rice into 6 equal portions. Put a sheet of nori shiny-side down on a rolling mat with the longest end towards you and, using wet hands, spread 1 portion of the rice in an even layer on the nori, leaving 2 cm/3/4 inch of nori visible at the end farthest away from you.

Spread a small amount of wasabi onto the rice at the end nearest you. Lay an asparagus spear on top of the wasabi, then put 2 pieces of crab next to it. Add a line of mushrooms.

To roll the sushi, fold the mat over, starting at the end where the ingredients are and tucking

in the end of the nori to start the roll. Keep rolling, lifting up the mat as you go and keeping the pressure even but gentle until you have finished the roll. Moisten the top edge of the nori with water to seal the sushi roll closed.

Remove the roll from the mat and cut it into 4 even-sized pieces with a wet, very sharp knife. Arrange the rolls on a plate. Repeat with the remaining ingredients and serve with the Ponzu Sauce.

SHIITAKE MUSHROOMS CAN BE BOUGHT BOTH FRESH AND DRIED. IF YOU CAN'T FIND THE FRESH MUSHROOMS, THEN SOAK DRIED ONES IN BOILING WATER FOR 30 MINUTES, DRAIN AND SQUEEZE DRY. YOU CAN NOW COOK THEM ACCORDING TO THE RECIPE.

# SEVEN-SPICED
## SALMON ROLLS

**MAKES 24 PIECES**

150-g/5¹/2-oz piece of salmon fillet

sichimi togarashi (seven-spice powder)

chilli flakes

1 tbsp oil

1 quantity freshly cooked sushi rice (see page 10)

6 small sheets of toasted nori

2 tbsp Japanese mayonnaise

*To serve*

shoyu (Japanese soy sauce)

wasabi paste

pickled ginger

Pull the skin off the salmon fillet and remove any bones. Dust the surface heavily with sichimi togarashi and sprinkle over a few chilli flakes. Heat the oil in a frying pan and cook the salmon over a medium heat on both sides for 8 minutes, or until it is cooked through. Cool and flake into large pieces.

Divide the rice into 6 equal portions. Put a sheet of nori shiny-side down on a rolling mat with the longest end towards you and, using wet hands, spread 1 portion of the rice in an even layer on the nori, leaving 2 cm/³/4 inch of nori visible at the end farthest away from you. Don't squash the rice or make the layer too thick – you should be able to see the nori through the rice.

Spread the mayonnaise onto the rice at the end nearest you. Lay a sixth of the salmon on top of the mayonnaise.

To roll the sushi, fold the mat over, starting at the end where the ingredients are and tucking in the end of the nori to start the roll. Keep rolling, lifting up the mat as you go and keeping the pressure even but gentle until you have finished the roll. Moisten the top edge of the nori with water to seal the sushi roll closed.

Remove the roll from the mat and cut it into 4 even-sized pieces with a wet, very sharp knife. Turn the pieces on end and arrange them on a plate. Repeat with the remaining ingredients. Serve with shoyu, wasabi and pickled ginger.

SICHIMI TOGARASHI IS A SEVEN-SPICE MIX USUALLY CONTAINING RED PEPPER, SANSHO PEPPER, SESAME SEEDS, FLAX SEEDS, POPPY SEEDS, GROUND NORI AND DRIED, GROUND TANGERINE PEEL.

# PORK
# TONKATSU ROLLS

**MAKES 24 PIECES**

2 tbsp flour

1 egg, lightly beaten

4 tbsp tonkatsu crumbs or dried white breadcrumbs

200 g/7 oz pork fillet, cut into thin slices

4 tbsp oil

1 quantity freshly cooked sushi rice (see page 10)

6 small sheets of toasted nori

2 tbsp Japanese mayonnaise

*To serve*

shoyu (Japanese soy sauce)

wasabi paste

pickled ginger

Put the flour, egg and crumbs in separate bowls. One by one, dust each piece of pork in the flour, dip it in the egg, then finally press it into the crumbs. Lay the breaded pork on a plate and chill for 20 minutes.

Heat the oil in a frying pan and fry the pork on both sides until the crumbs are a golden brown. It won't take long as the slices are quite thin. Cut the slices into strips.

Divide the rice into 6 equal portions. Put a sheet of nori shiny-side down on a rolling mat with the longest end towards you and, using wet hands, spread 1 portion of the rice in an even layer on the nori, leaving 2 cm/3/4 inch of nori visible at the end farthest away from you.

Spread the mayonnaise onto the rice at the end nearest you. Lay a sixth of the pork strips on top of the mayonnaise in a line.

To roll the sushi, fold the mat over, starting at the end where the ingredients are and tucking in the end of the nori to start the roll. Keep rolling, lifting up the mat as you go and keeping the pressure even but gentle until you have

finished the roll. Moisten the top edge of the nori with water to seal the sushi roll closed.

Remove the roll from the mat and cut it into 4 even-sized pieces with a wet, very sharp knife. Turn the pieces on end and arrange them on a plate. Repeat with the remaining ingredients. Serve with shoyu, wasabi and pickled ginger.

TONKATSU CRUMBS ARE TOASTED BREADCRUMBS, ALSO CALLED 'PANKO', WHICH ARE USED FOR COATING PORK FILLETS BEFORE FRYING THEM. THEY ABSORB LESS GREASE THAN NORMAL BREADCRUMBS, BUT YOU CAN USE COMMERCIAL PRE-TOASTED BREADCRUMBS INSTEAD.

# CHICKEN TERIYAKI ROLLS

**MAKES 24 PIECES**

1 chicken breast, cut into strips

2 tbsp teriyaki sauce

1 tbsp oil

1 quantity freshly cooked sushi rice (see page 10)

6 small sheets of toasted nori

5-cm/2-inch piece of cucumber, peeled and cut into batons

*To serve*

shoyu (Japanese soy sauce)

wasabi paste

pickled ginger

Preheat the grill to its highest setting. Toss the chicken in the teriyaki sauce and then the oil and lay out on a foil-lined grill pan. Grill the chicken strips on both sides for about 4 minutes, put into a bowl with any cooking juices and leave to cool.

Divide the rice into 6 equal portions. Put a sheet of nori shiny-side down on a rolling mat with the longest end towards you and, using wet hands, spread 1 portion of the rice in an even layer on the nori, leaving 2 cm/³/₄ inch of nori visible at the end farthest away from you. Don't squash the rice or make the layer too thick – you should be able to see the nori through the rice.

Lay the chicken strips in an even line onto the rice at the end nearest you. Add a line of cucumber batons.

To roll the sushi, fold the mat over, starting at the end where the ingredients are and tucking in the end of the nori to start the roll. Keep rolling, lifting up the mat as you go and keeping the pressure even but gentle until you have finished the roll. Moisten the top edge of the nori with water to seal the sushi roll closed. Don't worry if anything falls out of the sides, just push it back in. The edges may well look ragged, but don't worry.

Remove the roll from the mat and cut it into 4 even-sized pieces with a wet, very sharp knife. Turn the pieces on end and arrange them on a plate. Repeat with the remaining ingredients. Serve with shoyu, wasabi and pickled ginger.

TERIYAKI SAUCE IS A WIDELY AVAILABLE FLAVOURING, OR COOK-IN SAUCE. MADE FROM SOY SAUCE, MIRIN, SAKE, SUGAR AND GINGER. IT GIVES FOOD A GLOSSY COATING.

# PRAWN & AVOCADO SKEWERS

**MAKES 6**

1 quantity freshly cooked sushi rice (see page 10)

6 small sheets of toasted nori

1 tbsp Japanese mayonnaise

1 tsp lemon zest

12 cooked tiger prawns, peeled and deveined

2 ripe avocados, cut into strips

5-cm/2-inch piece of cucumber, peeled and cut into batons

6 bamboo skewers

Divide the rice into 6 equal portions. Put a sheet of nori shiny-side down on a rolling mat with the longest end towards you and, using wet hands, spread 1 portion of the rice in an even layer on the nori, leaving 2 cm/3/4 inch of nori visible at the end farthest away from you. Don't squash the rice or make the layer too thick – you should be able to see the nori through the rice.

Mix the mayonnaise with the lemon zest and spread some onto the rice at the end nearest to you. Lay 2 prawns end to end on top of the mayonnaise, then put a line of avocado next to them. Lay a line of cucumber next to the avocado.

To roll the sushi, fold the mat over, starting at the end where the ingredients are and tucking in the end of the nori to start the roll. Keep rolling, lifting up the mat as you go and keeping the pressure even but gentle until you have finished the roll. Moisten the top edge of the nori with water to seal the sushi roll closed. Don't worry if anything falls out of the sides, just push it back in. The edges may well look ragged, but don't worry.

Remove the roll from the mat and cut into 4 even-sized pieces with a wet, very sharp knife. If you don't use a sharp knife the roll will squash as you cut it. Lay the pieces on their side. Push each bamboo skewer through 4 pieces, making sure they are at the end so that you can eat them easily.

NORI SHEETS ARE MADE FROM DRIED LAVER SEAWEED AND COME IN DIFFERENT SIZES. IF YOU CAN FIND THEM IN BOTH LARGE AND SMALL SIZES, USE WHICHEVER IS APPROPRIATE TO THE RECIPE. IF YOU CAN ONLY FIND ONE SIZE, ADJUST THE RECIPE TO SUIT THE SIZE OF THE SHEET. BUY NORI SHEETS THAT ARE MARKED 'TOASTED' IF POSSIBLE. UN-TOASTED SHEETS ARE NOT AS CRISP OR HIGHLY FLAVOURED, BUT YOU CAN TOAST THEM BY PASSING THE NON-SHINY SIDE OVER A NAKED FLAME. WHEN ROLLING THE SHEETS, ALWAYS PUT THEM ON THE MAT SHINY-SIDE DOWN.

# INSIDE-OUT CALIFORNIA ROLLS

**MAKES 24 PIECES**

1 quantity freshly cooked sushi rice (see page 10)

6 small sheets of toasted nori

1/4 ripe avocado, cut into strips

5-cm/2-inch piece of cucumber, peeled and cut into batons

6 crab sticks, split in half lengthways

3 tbsp toasted sesame seeds

Divide the rice into 6 equal portions. Line a rolling mat with clingfilm to prevent the rice sticking to it. Put a sheet of nori shiny-side down on the mat with the longest end towards you. Using wet hands, spread 1 portion of the rice in an even layer on the nori, leaving no gaps, then turn the nori over so that the mat is against the rice.

Put some avocado in a layer at one end of the roll, keeping it parallel to the edge nearest you, and lay 2 pieces of crab in a line beside it. Put a line of cucumber next to them.

To roll the sushi, fold the mat over, starting at the end where the ingredients are and tucking in the end of the nori to start the roll. Keep rolling, lifting up the mat as you go and keeping the pressure even but gentle until you have finished the roll. Put the sesame seeds on a plate and roll the sushi in them to coat the rice.

Remove the roll from the mat and cut it into 4 even-sized pieces with a wet, very sharp knife. If you don't use a sharp knife the roll will squash as you cut it. Turn the pieces on end and arrange them on a plate. Repeat with the remaining ingredients.

SESAME SEEDS ARE AVAILABLE RAW AND TOASTED, THE TOASTED ONES HAVING A MORE PRONOUNCED FLAVOUR. IF YOU CAN ONLY FIND RAW ONES, THEN DRY-FRY THEM IN A HOT FRYING PAN UNTIL THEY BROWN AND START TO SMELL AROMATIC.

# INSIDE-OUT ROLLS
## WITH BEEF TERIYAKI

**MAKES 24 PIECES**

150 g/5¹/₂ oz fillet steak, trimmed

2 tbsp teriyaki sauce

1 tbsp oil

1 quantity freshly cooked sushi rice (see page 10)

6 small sheets of toasted nori

2 spring onions, shredded

3 tbsp toasted sesame seeds

Beat the steak out flat using a meat mallet or rolling pin to make it thinner and more tender. Coat the steak in the teriyaki sauce and leave it to marinate for an hour. Heat the oil in a frying pan and cook the steak for 3 minutes on each side. Cut the steak into thin strips.

Divide the rice into 6 equal portions. Line a rolling mat with clingfilm to prevent the rice sticking to it. Put a sheet of nori shiny-side down on the mat with the longest end towards you and, using wet hands, spread 1 portion of the rice in an even layer on the nori, leaving no gaps, then turn the nori over so that the mat is against the rice. Put a sixth of the beef teriyaki in a layer at one long end of the roll, top with a layer of spring onion and sprinkle with a few sesame seeds.

To roll the sushi, fold the mat over, starting at the end where the ingredients are and tucking in the end of the nori to start the roll. Keep rolling, lifting up the mat as you go and keeping the pressure even but gentle until you have finished the roll. Put the remaining sesame seeds on a plate and roll the sushi in them to coat the rice.

Remove the roll from the mat and cut it into 4 even-sized pieces with a wet, very sharp knife. If you don't use a sharp knife the roll will squash as you cut it. Turn the pieces on end and arrange them on a plate. Repeat with the remaining ingredients.

THIS RECIPE WORKS EQUALLY WELL WITH CHICKEN, SALMON OR SLICES OF TOFU. USE THE SAME WEIGHT OF ANY OF THE ABOVE AND FOLLOW THE RECIPE IN THE SAME WAY.

These are the two easiest styles of sushi to make as they involve no rolling or shaping by hand. Pressed sushi and box sushi, *oshi-zushi* and *hako-zushi*, are made in a three-piece bamboo pressing box called an *oshi waku*, but a loose-bottomed cake tin or terrine tin with drop-down sides will work just as well. If you only have fixed-base tins, then make the sushi upside-down, putting the toppings into the bottom of the tin, pressing the rice on top, then simply turning the sushi out. If you arrange your toppings in diagonal strips and cut the sushi into bar shapes, you will end up with an interesting striped effect. Once you have turned the sushi out, wait for a few minutes before cutting it to allow the flavours to develop. You will need to use a very sharp knife, wiped with a damp cloth between each cut, to keep it neat.

Scattered sushi, *chirashi-zushi*, is sometimes called 'housewives' sushi' because this is the type

# PART TWO PRESSED & SCATTERED SUSHI

most commonly made at home in Japan. All you need to make this is an attractive serving bowl for each person eating it. Red and black lacquered wooden bowls look wonderful, but you can use any bowl. Some suggested toppings are given in this chapter, but you can treat scattered sushi as you would a rice salad and mix and match the toppings as you like. You can add some pickled ginger and wasabi to the topping as a garnish or serve them separately in little bowls alongside some soy sauce and mayonnaise for dipping.

# SALMON, LEMON MAYONNAISE & AVOCADO PRESSED SUSHI BARS

**MAKES 8–10 PIECES**

¹/₂ quantity freshly cooked sushi rice (see page 10)

2 tbsp Japanese mayonnaise

2 tsp lemon zest

150 g/5¹/₂ oz smoked salmon

1 large ripe avocado, cut into thin batons

*To serve*

pickled ginger

wasabi paste

Oil an *oshi waku* or terrine tin (preferably with drop-down sides) and line it with a piece of clingfilm so that the clingfilm hangs over the edges. This is to help you pull the sushi out afterwards. Pack the tin 3 cm/1¹/₄ inches full with the rice. Mix the mayonnaise with the lemon zest and spread a layer of mayonnaise on top of the rice. Arrange the smoked salmon and avocado in thick, diagonal strips on top of the rice. Cover the top of the rice with a strip of clingfilm, put another terrine tin on top and add something heavy, such as a couple of tins of tomatoes, to weigh it down.

Chill the sushi for 15 minutes, then take off the tin and weights and pull out the sushi. Cut the sushi into 8–10 pieces with a wet, sharp knife. Serve with pickled ginger and wasabi paste.

OSHI WAKU ARE
WOODEN BOXES MADE
FOR PRESSING SUSHI.
THEY CONSIST OF
A FRAME PLUS A
REMOVABLE LID AND
BASE AND COME IN
DIFFERENT SIZES.

# TERIYAKI TUNA PRESSED SUSHI WITH GREEN BEAN STRIPS

**MAKES 15 PIECES**

200 g/7 oz sushi-grade tuna or tuna fillet, thinly sliced

2 tbsp teriyaki sauce

1 tbsp oil

10 green beans, topped, tailed and cut in half

oil, for frying

1 tsp toasted sesame seeds

1/2 quantity freshly cooked sushi rice (see page 10)

2 tbsp Japanese mayonnaise

*To serve*

pickled ginger

wasabi paste

Coat the tuna slices in the teriyaki sauce and fry in the oil in a frying pan for 1 minute on each side. Then cut them into thick strips. Blanch the green beans in boiling water for a minute, then cool under cold running water and drain.

Oil an *oshi waku* or 18-cm/7-inch loose-bottomed square cake tin and line it with a piece of clingfilm so that the clingfilm hangs over the edges. This is to help you pull the sushi out afterwards. Oil the clingfilm and scatter in the sesame seeds. Pack the tin 3 cm/1 1/4 inches full with the rice. Spread a layer of mayonnaise on top. Arrange the tuna and green beans in thick, diagonal strips on top of the rice. Cover the top of the rice with a strip of clingfilm, put another cake tin on top and weight down with something heavy, such as a couple of tins of tomatoes.

Let the sushi chill for about 15 minutes, then take off the tin and weights, loosen

the sides of the tin and pull out the sushi. Cut the sushi into about 15 pieces with a wet, sharp knife. Serve with pickled ginger and wasabi paste.

PICKLED GINGER SLICES ARE USED TO CLEANSE THE PALATE IN BETWEEN EATING DIFFERENT TYPES OF SUSHI. PICKLED GINGER CAN BE BOUGHT IN BAGS AND IS OFTEN A BRIGHT PINK COLOUR.

# PRESSED SUSHI BARS WITH SMOKED SALMON & CUCUMBER

**MAKES 8–10 PIECES**

¹/₂ quantity freshly cooked sushi rice (see page 10)

2 tbsp Japanese mayonnaise

200 g/7 oz smoked salmon

¹/₂ cucumber, peeled and cut into very thin slices

*To garnish*

2 lemons, cut into wedges

handful of mint sprigs

Oil an *oshi waku* or terrine tin (preferably with drop-down sides) and line it with a piece of clingfilm so that the clingfilm hangs over the edges. This is to help you pull the sushi out afterwards. Pack the tin 3 cm/1 ¹/₄ inches full with the rice. Spread a layer of mayonnaise on top of the rice. Arrange the smoked salmon and cucumber in diagonal strips on top of the rice, doubling up the smoked salmon layers if you have enough so that the topping is nice and thick. Cover the top of the rice with a strip of clingfilm, put another terrine tin on top and add something heavy, such as a couple of tins of tomatoes, to weight it down.

Chill the sushi for 15 minutes, then take off the tin and weights and pull out the sushi. Cut the sushi into 8–10 pieces with a wet, sharp knife. Garnish with lemon wedges and mint sprigs.

SMOKED SALMON MAKES A GOOD INGREDIENT IN SUSHI BECAUSE OF ITS TEXTURE. YOU CAN BUY A PIECE OF FILLET AND SLICE IT YOURSELF IF YOU WANT THICKER SLICES.

# PRESSED
# CALIFORNIA SUSHI

**MAKES 15 PIECES**

¹/₂ quantity freshly cooked sushi rice (see page 10)

2 tbsp Japanese mayonnaise

1 tsp toasted sesame seeds

¹/₂ avocado, cut into strips

4 crab sticks, sliced on the diagonal, or the flesh from a cooked, prepared crab

¹/₂ cucumber, peeled and cut into very thin slices

*To garnish*

lemon slices

dill

pickled ginger

wasabi paste

Oil an *oshi waku* or 18-cm/7-inch loose-bottomed square cake tin and line it with a piece of clingfilm so that the clingfilm hangs over the edges. This is to help you pull the sushi out afterwards. Pack the tin 3 cm/1¹/₄ inches full with the rice. Spread a layer of mayonnaise on top of the rice and sprinkle over the sesame seeds. Arrange the avocado, crab and cucumber in thick, diagonal strips on top of the rice. Cover the top of the rice with a strip of clingfilm, put another cake tin on top and add something heavy, such as a couple of tins of tomatoes, to weight it down.

Chill the sushi for 15 minutes, then take off the tin and weights, loosen the sides of the tin and pull out the sushi. Cut the sushi into about 15 pieces with a wet, sharp knife. Serve garnished with lemon, dill, pickled ginger and a dab of wasabi paste.

WASABI IS USUALLY BOUGHT AS A PASTE OR POWDER AND IS MADE FROM A GRATED ROOT. THE POWDER CAN BE MIXED TO A PASTE AND IS OFTEN OF A BETTER QUALITY THAN THE TUBES OF PASTE. WASABI GETS RID OF ANY FISHINESS IN SUSHI, BUT IT IS VERY STRONG SO BE CAREFUL NOT TO USE TOO MUCH.

# MEDITERRANEAN
# PRESSED SUSHI

**MAKES 15 PIECES**

2 red peppers

$^1$/$_2$ quantity freshly cooked sushi rice (see page 10)

oil, for brushing

4 sun-dried tomatoes in oil, drained and cut into strips

100 g/3$^1$/$_2$ oz mozzarella, cut into thin slices

handful of small basil leaves

Preheat the oven to 200°C/400°F/Gas Mark 6. Put the peppers in a roasting tin and cook them for 30 minutes, or until the skins have browned and started to puff away from the flesh. Cool, then pull off the skins. Cut each pepper in half and discard the stalk, seeds and membrane. Cut the peppers into strips.

Oil an *oshi waku* or 18-cm/7-inch loose-bottomed square cake tin and line it with a piece of clingfilm so that the clingfilm hangs over the edges. This is to help you pull the sushi out afterwards. Pack the tin 3 cm/1$^1$/$_4$ inches full with the rice and brush the top with a tiny amount of oil to help the toppings stick.

Arrange the pepper and mozzarella in thick, diagonal strips on top of the rice, alternating green basil leaves and red sun-dried tomatoes as thinner strips between the thick pepper and mozzarella strips. Cover the top of the rice with a strip of clingfilm, put another tin or flat tray on top and add something heavy, such as a couple of tins of tomatoes, to weight it down.

Chill the sushi for 15 minutes, then take off the tin and weights, loosen the sides of the tin and pull out the sushi. Cut the sushi into about 15 pieces with a wet, sharp knife.

WEIGHT DOWN PRESSED SUSHI BY APPLYING A FIRM, EVEN PRESSURE SO THAT THE DECORATIVE LAYER STAYS FLAT. THE INGREDIENTS CAN BE ARRANGED IN THE BOTTOM AND THE RICE PRESSED ON TOP, OR THE OTHER WAY AROUND.

# SCATTERED SUSHI
## WITH SMOKED MACKEREL

**SERVES 4**

8 mangetout

5-cm/2-inch piece of daikon

1 quantity freshly cooked sushi rice (see page 10)

juice and zest of 1 lemon

2 spring onions, finely chopped

2 smoked mackerel, skin removed and cut into diagonal strips

1/2 cucumber, peeled and cut into slices

*To garnish*

pickled ginger

strips of toasted nori

wasabi paste

DAIKON IS A LONG,
WHITE RADISH THAT
HAS A CRISP WHITE
FLESH AND A PEPPERY
FLAVOUR. IT GOES
WELL WITH FISH
AND IS OFTEN USED
AS A GARNISH.

Cook the mangetout in boiling, salted water for 1 minute. Drain and put aside to cool. Shred the daikon using the finest setting on a mandolin or a very sharp knife. If you are using a knife, then cut the daikon into long, thin slices and cut each slice along its length as finely as you can.

Mix the sushi rice with the lemon juice and lemon zest.

Divide the rice between 4 wooden or ceramic bowls – they should be about 2 cm/ 3/4 inch full. Scatter the spring onion over the top. Arrange the mackerel, cucumber, mangetout and daikon on top of the rice. Garnish with pickled ginger, nori strips and a small mound of wasabi.

# SCATTERED SUSHI WITH SOY-GLAZED STEAK

**SERVES 4**

8 dried shiitake mushrooms

5-cm/2-inch piece of daikon, peeled

5-cm/2-inch piece of carrot, peeled

1 tbsp soy sauce

1 tsp mirin

1 tsp brown sugar

200 g /7 oz fillet steak, trimmed

1 quantity freshly cooked sushi rice (see page 10)

*To garnish*

strips of toasted nori

wasabi paste

*To serve*

pickled ginger

Soak the mushrooms in boiling water for 20 minutes, then simmer them in the same liquid for 3 minutes. Lift them out and squeeze them dry. Chop 4 mushrooms into small pieces and halve the rest. Shred the daikon and carrot using the finest setting on a mandolin or a very sharp knife. If you are using a knife, then cut the daikon and carrot into long, thin slices and cut each slice along its length as finely as you can.

Preheat the grill to its highest setting. Mix the soy sauce, mirin and brown sugar together and brush the mixture all over the steak. Grill the steak for 3 minutes on each side, then leave it to rest for a minute. Slice into strips.

Mix the sushi rice with the chopped shiitake mushrooms.

Fill 1 large or 4 small wooden or ceramic bowls or plates with the rice – they should be about 2 cm/³/4 inch full. Arrange the steak and

halved mushrooms on top of the rice and add a neat pile of shredded daikon and carrot to each bowl. Garnish with some nori strips and a small mound of wasabi. Serve the pickled ginger on the side.

MIRIN IS A SWEET RICE WINE THAT ACTS AS A FLAVOURING. IT IS USED TO MAKE SUSHI RICE AND GIVES A LUSTRE TO THE RICE AS WELL AS ADDING FLAVOUR. HON MIRIN AND SHIN MIRIN ARE THE 2 VARIETIES, THE DIFFERENCE BEING THAT HON MIRIN CONTAINS MORE ALCOHOL.

# SCATTERED SUSHI WITH PRAWNS, CRAB & AVOCADO

**SERVES 4**

6 large raw prawns, peeled and deveined

1 tbsp oil

1 cooked prepared crab

1 quantity freshly cooked sushi rice (see page 10)

juice and zest of 1 lemon

1 ripe avocado, cut into strips

1/2 cucumber, peeled and cut into slices

IF YOU WOULD LIKE TO KEEP THE PRAWNS STRAIGHT SO THAT THEY ARE EASIER TO ARRANGE IN LINES, THEN PUSH A SKEWER THROUGH THEIR LENGTH BEFORE COOKING TO STOP THEM CURLING UP.

Cook the prawns by frying them for 2 minutes on each side in the oil. Once they are cooked, cool and cut in half lengthways. Lift the crabmeat out of the shell.

Mix the sushi rice with the lemon juice and lemon zest.

Divide the rice between 4 wooden or ceramic bowls – they should be about 2 cm/ 3/4 inch full. Arrange the prawns, crab, avocado and cucumber on top of the rice.

# SCATTERED SUSHI WITH LOBSTER & WASABI MAYONNAISE

**SERVES 4**

1 cooked lobster

2 tbsp Japanese mayonnaise

1 tsp wasabi paste

1 quantity freshly cooked sushi rice (see page 10)

1 tbsp pickled ginger, very finely chopped

$1/2$ cucumber, cut into slices

1 ripe avocado, cut into slices

*To garnish*

wasabi paste

pickled ginger

Take the meat out of the lobster shell in as big pieces as you can. If your lobster is whole, the best way to do this is to twist off the head and halve the body down the centre with a big sharp knife or cleaver. The claws will have to be smashed open to get at the meat. Cover them with a cloth and hit them hard with a rolling pin.

Mix the mayonnaise with the wasabi. Mix the sushi rice with the finely chopped pickled ginger.

Divide the rice between 4 wooden or ceramic bowls – they should be about 2 cm/ $3/4$ inch full. Arrange the lobster, cucumber and avocado on top of the rice and drizzle the wasabi mayonnaise into the gaps. Garnish with pickled ginger and a small mound of wasabi.

LOBSTER CAN BE BOUGHT COOKED, BUT IF YOU PLAN ON COOKING IT YOURSELF THEN MAKE SURE THAT YOU BUY IT LIVE.

# COCKTAIL SCATTERED
# SUSHI ON SCALLOP SHELLS

**MAKES 8 SHELLS**

8 scallops with their shells

1 tbsp oil

juice and zest of $^1/_2$ lime

$^1/_3$ quantity freshly cooked
sushi rice (see page 10)

handful of fresh coriander
leaves

*To garnish*

pickled ginger

wasabi paste

3 tbsp Japanese mayonnaise

Remove the scallops from their shells and clean
and keep the shells for serving. Clean the
scallops by pulling off the small, white shiny

SCALLOPS CAN BE
BOUGHT ON THE SHELL
AND THE FISHMONGER
MAY EVEN BE ABLE TO
CLEAN THEM FOR
YOU. PACKETS OF
SCALLOP SHELLS CAN
ALSO BE BOUGHT FOR
DECORATIVE PURPOSES.

muscle and its membrane. Leave the roe
attached, but check to see if there is a black
vein that needs to be cut off – this is easiest
with a pair of scissors. Heat the oil in a frying
pan and briefly fry the scallops on both sides
until they are lightly browned and cooked
through. Squeeze a little of the lime juice over
each scallop and cool.

Mix the sushi rice with the remaining lime
juice and zest.

Divide the rice between 8 scallop shells –
make a small, neat mound on each one and
flatten the top a little. Arrange a scallop along
with a few coriander leaves on top of the rice
in each shell, then garnish with a piece of
pickled ginger, a tiny mound of wasabi and a
dollop of mayonnaise. Serve on a platter with
a pile of chopsticks.

Hand-rolled sushi, *temaki*, make perfect snacks. They are big enough to need more than one bite and are reasonably filling. Boat sushi, *gunkanmaki*, make a nice addition to a sushi platter as they vary the shapes you are using.

Legend has it that hand rolls were invented so that Japanese gangsters could eat while they were playing cards. The rolls are designed to be eaten with your hands and are very easy to pick up. They are best made at the last minute so that the nori stays crisp. Hand rolls can be served ready-made or, if you prefer, you can serve up the rice and fillings in bowls. Give each one of your guests a pile of nori squares and let them roll up their own. It is best to put a smear of

# PART THREE IT'S A WRAP

wasabi into the roll as you make it and sprinkle some drops of soy into the roll before you eat it as they are hard to dip successfully. Mini hand rolls using smaller nori squares make good canapés.

Boat sushi are made by wrapping a piece of nori around a moulded piece of rice. They are the best shape of sushi for serving toppings such as fish roe or slightly softer mixtures such as tuna mayonnaise or egg mayonnaise. Ready-made sandwich fillings or salad toppings are also good fillings for these and the rice base will absorb any excess sauce. You can vary the size of boat sushi, but pieces that take one or two bites are best.

# SWEET CHILLI SALMON HAND ROLLS

**MAKES 6 PIECES**

150-g/5¹/₂-oz piece of salmon fillet, skin on

salt and pepper

1 tbsp oil

¹/₄ quantity freshly cooked sushi rice (see page 10)

3 large sheets of toasted nori, halved

2 spring onions, halved and shredded

4 tbsp Japanese mayonnaise

2 tbsp sweet chilli sauce

*To serve*

cucumber batons

Season the piece of salmon with the salt and pepper. Heat the oil in a frying pan until it is very hot, then add the salmon skin-side down. Cook for 2 minutes until the skin is very crisp, then turn the heat down to medium and cook for a further 2 minutes. Turn the salmon over and cook for a further minute, or until it is cooked through. Leave to cool, then flake the salmon, keeping some pieces attached to the crispy skin.

Lay a piece of nori out on the work surface and put some rice on the sheet. Spread the rice out evenly so that it takes up the bottom two-thirds of the sheet. Lay a sixth of the salmon, salmon skin and spring onion on the rice, then drizzle over a little mayonnaise and dot on a tiny amount of sweet chilli sauce. Roll the nori into a cone, folding the bottom corner in as you roll. You will have to paste the join together with a couple of crushed grains of rice. Repeat with the other pieces of nori. Garnish with cucumber.

Sweet chilli sauce is available in many different brands. The best are Thai brands, available from Chinese and Thai shops.

# SALT & PEPPER
# SQUID HAND ROLLS

**MAKES 6 PIECES**

12 squid rings

4 tbsp plain flour

1 tsp Sichuan pepper or
black pepper, crushed

1 tsp sea salt, crushed

oil, for frying

3 large sheets of toasted
nori, halved

1/4 quantity freshly cooked
sushi rice (see page 10)

4 tbsp Japanese mayonnaise

Pull any membranes off the squid rings, then cut each one in half. Mix the flour with the Sichuan pepper and salt and put it with the squid in a plastic bag. Shake well until the squid is thoroughly coated.

Heat about 2 cm/3/4 inch of oil in a wok until it is very hot, then add the squid in batches and fry, stirring, for a minute, or until the coating is browned. Drain on kitchen paper to get rid of any excess oil.

Lay a piece of nori out on the work surface and put some rice on the sheet. Spread the rice out evenly so that it takes up the bottom two-thirds of the sheet. Lay a sixth of the salt and pepper squid on the rice, then drizzle over a little mayonnaise. Roll the nori into a cone, folding the bottom corner in as you roll. You will have to paste the join together with a couple of crushed grains of rice. Repeat with the other pieces of nori.

SICHUAN PEPPER IS NOT
A REAL PEPPER, BUT IS
MADE FROM THE RED
BERRIES OF THE PRICKLY
ASH TREE. THE JAPANESE
VERSION IS CALLED
SANSHO AND IS
INTERCHANGEABLE.

# COD GOUJON HAND ROLLS WITH TARTARE SAUCE

**MAKES 6 PIECES**

6 cod or haddock goujons

3 large sheets of toasted nori, halved

¹/4 quantity freshly cooked sushi rice (see page 10)

3 tbsp tartare sauce, plus extra to serve

3 spring onions, halved and shredded

Cook the goujons according to the packet instructions, cool, then cut into 4-cm/ 1¹/2-inch pieces.

Lay a piece of nori out on the work surface and put some rice on the sheet. Spread the rice out evenly so that it takes up the bottom two-thirds of the sheet. Spread a little of the tartare sauce onto the rice and top with a sixth of the goujons and spring onion. Roll the nori into a cone, folding the bottom corner in as you roll. You will have to paste the join together with a couple of crushed grains of rice. Repeat with the other pieces of nori. Serve with extra tartare sauce for dipping.

TARTARE SAUCE CAN BE EASILY BOUGHT, JUST LOOK FOR A PREMIUM BRAND BASED ON A WHOLE EGG MAYONNAISE FOR THE BEST FLAVOUR. IF YOU DON'T LIKE TARTARE SAUCE, THEN USE MAYONNAISE WITH THIS RECIPE.

# DUCK & HOISIN HAND ROLLS

**MAKES 6 PIECES**

¹/₄ barbecued or Peking duck

4 tbsp hoisin or plum sauce

3 large sheets of toasted nori, halved

¹/₄ quantity freshly cooked sushi rice (see page 10)

2 spring onions, halved and shredded, and extra to garnish

Pull the flesh and skin off the duck in big pieces, then slice these into strips. If you have lots of skin, then just keep the crispiest bits. Get rid of any excess fat. Toss the duck flesh and skin with half the hoisin or plum sauce.

Lay a piece of nori out on the work surface and put some rice on the sheet. Spread the rice out evenly so that it takes up the bottom two-thirds of the sheet. Lay a sixth of the duck, duck skin and spring onion on the rice, then drizzle over a little more of the hoisin or plum sauce. Roll the nori into a cone, folding the bottom corner in as you roll. You will have to paste the join together with a couple of crushed grains of rice. Repeat with the other pieces of nori. Garnish with shredded spring onions.

BARBECUED DUCK CAN BE BOUGHT FROM CHINESE RESTAURANTS WHERE YOU WILL SEE IT HANGING IN THE WINDOW. YOU CAN ALSO BUY IT FROM SUPERMARKETS ALONGSIDE THE CHINESE READY-MEALS. A ROASTED DUCK BREAST WILL ALSO WORK FOR THIS RECIPE.

# TUNA TATAKI HAND ROLLS

**MAKES 6 PIECES**

1 tsp black pepper

1 tbsp grated fresh ginger

1 tbsp sesame seeds

150 g/5¹/₂ oz sushi-grade tuna or very fresh tuna fillet

salt

2 tbsp oil

3 large sheets of toasted nori, halved

¹/₄ quantity freshly cooked sushi rice (see page 10)

¹/₂ cucumber, cut into batons

4 tbsp Japanese mayonnaise

wasabi paste

Mix the black pepper, ginger and sesame seeds together and rub them all over the tuna, pressing the seeds on firmly. Season the tuna lightly with salt. Heat the oil in a frying pan until it is very hot. Sear the tuna on all sides for 6 minutes, or until it is almost cooked through – keep pressing it until it feels firm. Remove from the pan, cool, then slice into thin slices.

Lay out a piece of nori on the work surface and put some rice on the sheet. Spread the rice out evenly so that it takes up the bottom two-thirds of the sheet. Lay a sixth of the tuna and cucumber on the rice, then drizzle over a little mayonnaise and dot on a tiny amount of wasabi. Roll the nori into a cone, folding the bottom corner in as you roll. You will have to paste the join together with a couple of crushed grains of rice. Repeat with the other pieces of nori.

HAND ROLLS CAN BE MADE IN DIFFERENT SIZES. THEY SHOULD IDEALLY BE BIG ENOUGH TO NEED SEVERAL BITES, BUT YOU CAN MAKE SMALLER COCKTAIL-SIZED ROLLS IF YOU PREFER.

# GLAZED EEL
# HAND ROLLS

**MAKES 6 PIECES**

125 ml/4¹/₂ fl oz soy sauce

2 tbsp mirin

2 tbsp sake

honey, to taste

3 large sheets of toasted
nori, halved

¹/₄ quantity freshly cooked
sushi rice (see page 10)

2 smoked eel fillets, cut into
strips lengthways

¹/₂ ripe avocado, cut into
slices

Put the soy sauce, mirin and sake in a saucepan
and simmer for 5 minutes, or until slightly
thickened. Stir in a teaspoon of honey, then
taste, adding more honey until the sauce is
sweet enough for you.

Lay out a piece of nori on the work surface
and put some rice on the sheet. Spread the rice
out evenly so that it takes up the bottom two-
thirds of the sheet. Lay a sixth of the eel over
the rice and drizzle the eel and rice liberally
with the sauce. Add a couple of slices of
avocado. Roll the nori into a cone, folding the
bottom corner in as you roll. You will have to
paste the join together with a couple of
crushed grains of rice. Repeat with the other
pieces of nori.

THE EEL (UNAGI) USED
FOR SUSHI HAS A SOY,
SAKE AND MIRIN GLAZE
BRUSHED OVER IT
BEFORE COOKING. YOU
CAN BUY GLAZED EEL
FROM JAPANESE SHOPS,
OR YOU CAN USE
SMOKED EEL FILLETS,
WHICH MAY BE EASIER
TO FIND.

# SALMON ROE SUSHI BOATS

**MAKES 8 PIECES**

¹/₃ quantity freshly cooked sushi rice (see page 10)

2 small sheets of toasted nori, each cut into 4 strips lengthways

wasabi paste

8 tbsp salmon, trout or flying fish roe

*To serve*

soy sauce

pickled ginger

Divide the rice into 8 batches. Dampen your hands to stop the rice sticking, then shape each batch of the rice into an oval using your hands. Carefully wrap a strip of nori around each piece

of rice, trim off any excess, then stick together at the join using a couple of crushed grains of rice.

Dab a little wasabi on top of each sushi boat and top with a tablespoon of the salmon roe. Serve the sushi straight away with soy sauce and pickled ginger on the side.

ROE IS OFTEN USED FOR MAKING SUSHI. MOST ROE USED IS ORANGE, EITHER LARGE SALMON OR TROUT ROE OR TINY FLYING FISH ROE. IT CAN BE BOUGHT IN JARS.

# GREEN BEAN SUSHI BOATS

**MAKES 8 PIECES**

20 green beans, topped, tailed and finely sliced

1 tbsp sesame oil

1 tbsp toasted sesame seeds

salt and pepper

1 tsp grated lemon zest

1/3 quantity freshly cooked sushi rice (see page 10)

2 small sheets of toasted nori, each cut into 4 strips lengthways

wasabi paste

*To serve*

soy sauce

pickled ginger

Put the green beans in a saucepan with a little water and bring to the boil. Cook for 2 minutes, then drain and toss with the sesame oil and sesame seeds. Season with salt and pepper to taste and mix in the lemon zest.

Divide the rice into 8 batches. Dampen your hands to stop the rice sticking, then shape each batch into an oval using your hands. Carefully wrap a strip of nori around each piece of rice, trim off any excess, then stick together at the join using a couple of crushed grains of rice.

Dab a little wasabi on top of each sushi boat and top with the green beans. Serve the sushi straight away with soy sauce and pickled ginger on the side.

BEAN SHREDDERS ARE THE BEST WAY TO SHRED BEANS INTO LONG STRIPS. THEY ARE SMALL PLASTIC FRAMES FILLED WITH 5 OR 6 BLADES.

# SMOKED TROUT SUSHI BOATS

**MAKES 8 PIECES**

¹/₃ quantity freshly cooked sushi rice (see page 10)

2 small sheets of toasted nori, each cut into 4 strips lengthways

2 tbsp Japanese mayonnaise

1 tsp grated lemon zest

2 tsp lemon juice

2 spring onions, finely chopped

1 smoked trout fillet, flaked

55 g/2 oz smoked salmon, cut into strips

*To serve*

Ponzu Sauce

4 radishes, finely chopped

SMOKED TROUT CAN BE BOUGHT AS FILLETS OR AS WHOLE TROUT. THE WHOLE TROUT OFTEN HAVE A MORE PRONOUNCED FLAVOUR.

Divide the rice into 8 batches. Dampen your hands to stop the rice sticking, then shape each batch of the rice into an oval using your hands. Carefully wrap a strip of nori around each piece of rice, trim off any excess, then stick together at the join using a couple of crushed grains of rice.

Mix the mayonnaise with the lemon zest and juice and spread a little on top of each sushi boat. Sprinkle with some spring onion, then top with some of the smoked trout and smoked salmon. Serve the sushi straight away with Ponzu sauce and chopped radish.

# LEMON PEPPER
# CRAB SUSHI BOATS

**MAKES 8 PIECES**

1 small cooked prepared crab

1 tsp grated lemon zest

1 tsp black pepper

2 tbsp Japanese mayonnaise

salt

1/3 quantity freshly cooked sushi rice (see page 10)

2 small sheets of toasted nori, each cut into 4 strips lengthways

juice of 1 lemon

*To garnish*

2 lemons, cut into wedges

Lift the crabmeat out of the shell and mix with the lemon, black pepper and mayonnaise. Season with salt to taste.

Divide the rice into 8 batches. Dampen your hands to stop the rice sticking, then shape each batch of the rice into an oval using your hands. Carefully wrap a strip of nori around each piece of rice, trim off any excess, then stick the seaweed together at the join using a couple of crushed grains of rice.

Top each sushi boat with some of the crab mixture and squeeze over a few drops of lemon juice. Serve the sushi straight away with lemon wedges on the side.

TO MAKE A REALLY QUICK AND EASY TOPPING, USE A TIN OF LEMON PEPPER TUNA INSTEAD OF THE CRAB. DRAIN THE TIN OF ANY EXCESS LIQUID AND STIR IT WELL BEFORE USE.

Sushi is becoming more and more inventive. Toppings are no longer restricted to raw fish and other Japanese-style ingredients; the traditional filling of rice is being replaced by noodles or even potato and egg; while red pepper and other ingredients are replacing the nori wrapping. Modern Japanese restaurants and sushi bars serve up new ideas on a daily basis and sushi appears on the menus of all sorts of other types of eating establishments. Sushi is no longer just Japanese; it is part of the modern dining experience. Traditionally, hot or cold sake or green tea is served with sushi and these two drinks go particularly well, but Japanese beer or wine also make a good accompaniment.

This chapter contains a few extra dishes that are served at sushi bars. Tempura, crisp fried fish, seafood and vegetables make a great

# PART FOUR SUSHI LOUNGE

accompaniment to sushi because they have a completely different texture and flavour. You can use any type of fish or seafood, as well as most firm-textured vegetables that cook through quickly. Tempura needs to be served hot, so make it at the last minute. Miso soup is a traditional accompaniment to sushi. You can serve it at the start of the meal, alongside the sushi, or as a refreshing palate cleanser at the end.

All these sushi recipes make good starters for dinner parties or canapés to serve with drinks. Mix and match a few of the recipes, plus a few from other chapters, to make up individual plates or a large sushi platter. Serve alongside miso in tiny cups for sipping.

# SOBA
# NOODLE ROLLS

**MAKES 24 PIECES**

115 g/4 oz sushi-grade tuna or piece of tuna fillet

1 tbsp oil

100 g/3½ oz soba noodles, broken into pieces

1 spring onion, green part only, cut into thin slices

1 tbsp light soy sauce

½ tbsp rice wine vinegar

wasabi paste

1 tbsp pickled ginger, finely chopped

6 small sheets of toasted nori

½ cucumber, peeled and finely shredded

If using a piece of tuna fillet, heat the oil in a frying pan and sear the tuna on all sides for 6 minutes, or until it is almost cooked through. Cut the sushi or cooked tuna into strips.

Cook the soba noodles in a saucepan of boiling water until they are just cooked through, drain and rinse under cold running water. Drain thoroughly. Gently mix the soba noodles with

the spring onion, soy sauce, rice wine vinegar, a pinch of wasabi and the pickled ginger.

Divide the noodles into 6 equal portions. Put a sheet of nori shiny-side down on a rolling mat with the longest end towards you and mound 1 portion of the noodle mixture on the bottom third of the nori. Lay a sixth of the cucumber on top, then a layer of tuna strips.

To roll the sushi, fold the mat over, starting at the end where the ingredients are and tucking in the end of the nori to start the roll. Keep rolling, lifting up the mat as you go and keeping the pressure even but gentle until you have finished the roll. Moisten the top edge of the nori with water to seal the sushi roll closed. Don't worry if anything falls out of the sides, just push it back in.

Remove the roll from the mat and cut it into 4 even-sized pieces with a wet, very sharp knife. Turn the pieces on end and arrange them on a plate. Repeat the process with the remaining ingredients.

SOBA NOODLES ARE LONG, BROWNISH-GREY NOODLES MADE FROM BUCKWHEAT AND WHEAT FLOUR. THEY CAN BE EATEN HOT OR COLD, AS HERE.

# GRILLED SALMON,
## SPINACH & WASABI MASH ROLLS

**MAKES 24 PIECES**

2 large potatoes, peeled and cut into quarters

1 spring onion, finely chopped

wasabi paste

115 g/4 oz sushi-grade salmon or piece of salmon fillet

1 tbsp oil

salt

6 small sheets of toasted nori

handful of spinach leaves, stalks removed

Cook the potatoes in a saucepan of boiling salted water for 20–30 minutes, or until tender. Mash, then mix them with the spring onion and enough wasabi to give the mash a bit of a kick. Season with salt to taste. Chill for 30 minutes, or until the mash is very firm.

If using the salmon fillet, pull the skin off and remove any bones. Heat the oil in a frying pan and cook the salmon over a medium heat, on both sides, for 8 minutes or until it is cooked through. Cool and cut the sushi or cooked salmon into strips.

Divide the mash into 6 equal portions. Put a sheet of nori shiny-side down on a rolling mat with the longest end towards you and mound 1 portion of the mash on the bottom third of the nori. Lay a sixth of the spinach leaves on top, then a layer of salmon.

To roll the sushi, fold the mat over, starting at the end where the ingredients are and tucking in the end of the nori to start the roll. Keep rolling, lifting up the mat as you go and keeping

the pressure even but gentle until you have finished the roll. Moisten the top edge of the nori with water to seal the sushi roll closed.

Remove the roll from the mat and cut it into 4 even-sized pieces with a wet, very sharp knife. Turn the pieces on end and arrange them on a plate. Repeat with the remaining ingredients.

USE GOOD ALL-PURPOSE OR MASHING POTATOES LIKE KING EDWARDS OR DESIREE FOR THIS RECIPE. YOU WANT A SMOOTH, THICK MASH SO THE FILLING STAYS SOLID AND ROLLS EASILY.

# SCALLOP, MAYONNAISE, POTATO & SESAME ROLLS

**MAKES 24 PIECES**

2 large potatoes, peeled and cut into quarters

2 tbsp butter

salt and pepper

1 tbsp olive oil

8 large scallops, cleaned

6 sheets of toasted nori

2 tbsp Japanese mayonnaise

2 tbsp toasted sesame seeds

Cook the potatoes in a saucepan of boiling salted water for 20–30 minutes, or until tender. Mash with the butter and season well with the salt and pepper. Chill for 30 minutes, or until the mash is very firm.

Heat the oil in a frying pan and sauté the scallops on both sides for 2–3 minutes. Slice them thinly into 3 coin-shaped pieces and season with salt to taste.

Divide the mash into 6 equal portions. Put a sheet of nori shiny-side down on a rolling mat with the longest end towards you and mound 1 portion of the mash on the bottom third of the nori. Spread some mayonnaise on top, then sprinkle on some sesame seeds. Add a sixth of the scallop slices.

To roll the sushi, fold the mat over, starting at the end where the ingredients are and tucking in the end of the nori to start the roll. Keep rolling, lifting up the mat as you go and keeping the pressure even but gentle until you have finished the roll. Moisten the top edge of the nori with water to seal the sushi roll closed.

Remove the roll from the mat and cut it into 4 even-sized pieces with a wet, very sharp knife. Turn the pieces on end and arrange them on a plate. Repeat with the remaining ingredients.

THIS RECIPE ALSO WORKS WITH FIRM WHITE FISH OR SALMON FILLETS. USE THICK SLICES OF FILLET AND FRY, GRILL OR STEAM UNTIL IT IS JUST COOKED.

# SUSHI BAGS

**MAKES 8 PIECES**

4 aburage (fried beancurd sheets)

175 ml/6 fl oz dashi stock

3 tbsp soy sauce

2 tbsp caster sugar

1 tbsp sake

1/4 quantity freshly cooked sushi rice (see page 10)

1 tbsp toasted sesame seeds

Put the beancurd in a bowl and pour boiling water over it to remove any excess oil, drain and cool. Cut each piece in half and gently open out each half into a bag.

Combine the dashi stock, soy sauce, sugar and sake in a saucepan and bring to the boil, add the beancurd bags and simmer for 10–15 minutes until the liquid has almost all been absorbed. Remove from heat, drain and cool. Press any remaining liquid out of the bags with a clean tea towel – they should be moist but not wet.

Add the sesame seeds to the sushi rice and mix them in. Fill the bags with the rice mixture and fold over the tops to enclose them. Serve at room temperature.

ABURAGE ARE WRAPPERS MADE BY LIFTING THE SKIN OFF SOYA MILK AND DRYING IT. THE POUCHES ARE USED TO MAKE THIS INARI (STUFFED) SUSHI. SOME COME DRY, OTHERS ARE PRE-SEASONED.

# TUNA SESAME BLOCKS

**MAKES 12 PIECES**

8 x 6-cm (3$^1$/4 x 2$^1$/2-inch) piece centre-cut tuna fillet (ask for a piece 2 cm/ $^3$/4 inch thick)

2 tsp sesame oil

2 tbsp toasted sesame seeds

3 small sheets of nori, cut into 4 strips lengthways

2 tbsp oil

Cut the tuna into 12 cubes and roll the cubes in the sesame oil, followed by the sesame seeds.

Roll each cube in a sheet of nori, trimming off any excess so that the nori goes round the tuna once with only a little overlap. Moisten the edge of the nori with a little water to stick it down.

Heat the oil in a frying pan and put the cubes into the pan, standing them up on one nori-free end. Cook for 2 minutes, then turn over to cook the other nori-free end. The sesame seeds should be a dark brown, but not burnt, and the tuna should have cooked most of the way through, leaving a rare patch in the middle. If you prefer your tuna fully cooked, then just cook each end for a little longer.

SESAME OIL COMES IN 2 SORTS: PALE UNROASTED OIL, USUALLY MIDDLE EASTERN, OR DARK ROASTED OIL, USUALLY FROM ASIA OR CHINA. THE ROASTED OIL HAS A MUCH STRONGER FLAVOUR.

# ASPARAGUS & OMELETTE
## ROLLS WITH PONZU SAUCE

**MAKES 6–8 PIECES**

8 asparagus spears

4 eggs

I tbsp water

I tbsp mirin

I tsp soy sauce

1/2 tbsp oil

*To serve*

Ponzu Sauce (see page 16)

Lay the asparagus flat in a frying pan filled with simmering water and cook until tender when pierced with the tip of a knife. Leave to cool.

Whisk the eggs with the water, mirin and soy sauce. Heat the oil in a non-stick frying pan and pour in the egg mixture. Cook on one side until the top is just set, then add the asparagus spears by laying them in lines at one end of the pan.

Shake the pan to loosen the omelette. Now roll up the omelette, starting at the asparagus end, by tipping the pan away from you so that

the omelette slides up the side of the pan. Using 2 chopsticks, fold the omelette over and keep rolling it up like a Swiss roll.

Put a sheet of clingfilm in the centre of a rolling mat. Tip the omelette out onto the clingfilm and roll it up in the mat to help it set in shape. Leave to cool.

Remove the roll from the mat and cut it into 2-cm (3/4-inch) pieces with a wet, very sharp knife. Turn the pieces on end and arrange them on a plate. Serve with the Ponzu Sauce for dipping.

PONZU SAUCE IS TRADITIONALLY MADE WITH PONZU, OR KALAMANSI, AN ORIENTAL CITRON VARIETY. LEMON OR LIME JUICE CAN BE USED INSTEAD.

# PRAWN ROLLS

**MAKES 12 PIECES**

2 red peppers

1 small ripe avocado, cut into slices

8 large cooked peeled prawns

salt and pepper

Preheat the oven to 200°C/400°F/Gas Mark 6. Put the peppers in a roasting tin and cook them for 30 minutes, or until the skins have browned and started to puff away from the flesh. Cool, then pull off the skins. Cut each pepper in half and discard the stalk, seeds and membrane.

Lay out each pepper half on a board and make a pile of avocado slices at one end. Add

2 prawns to each and season well with salt and pepper. Roll up the peppers tightly, wrap each roll tightly in clingfilm and chill for 30 minutes.

Carefully unwrap the clingfilm from the peppers and trim each end until it is straight. Cut each into 3 pieces with a wet, very sharp knife. Turn the pieces on end and arrange them on a plate.

AVOCADO USED FOR SUSHI SHOULD BE FIRM AND RIPE, BUT NOT OVER-RIPE OR THE PRESSURE USED TO ROLL THE SUSHI WILL SQUASH IT.

# VEGETABLE & TOFU TEMPURA

**SERVES 4**

1 potato, peeled

1/4 butternut squash, peeled

1 small sweet potato, peeled

1 small aubergine

150 g/5 1/2 oz packet tempura mix

6 green beans, topped and tailed

1 red pepper, cut into thick strips

350 g/12 oz block firm tofu, cubed

6 whole shiitake or button mushrooms, stalks trimmed

1 stalk broccoli, broken into florets

oil, for deep-frying

few drops of sesame oil

*To serve*

sweet chilli sauce

Cut the potato, squash, sweet potato and aubergine into 1-cm/1/2-inch thick pieces.

Combine the tempura mix with the amount of water described on the packet instructions until you have a lumpy batter full of air bubbles. Do not try to make the batter smooth or it will be heavy, and make sure you use it straight away or it will settle.

Drop all the prepared vegetables and tofu into the batter.

Heat the oil in a deep-fryer to 180–190°C/ 350–375°F, or until a cube of bread browns in 30 seconds. Add a few drops of sesame oil.

Add the tempura in batches of 2–3. If you add too many pieces at one time the oil temperature will drop and the batter will be soggy. When the tempura pieces are a very light golden colour, which should take only 2–3 minutes, take them out and try to drain off as

much oil as possible. Leave them to drain on a piece of kitchen paper for 30 seconds to blot up more oil.

Serve this dish very hot with sweet chilli sauce.

TOFU IS SOLD IN CARTONS IN MOST SUPERMARKETS, BUT YOU WILL FIND A MUCH WIDER VARIETY IN JAPANESE OR CHINESE SHOPS. SILKEN TOFU IS VERY SOFT AND BREAKS EASILY, BUT HAS A WONDERFUL TEXTURE. FIRM TOFU IS HARDER AND EASIER TO USE. THERE IS A JAPANESE VERSION CALLED NIGARI.

# SEAFOOD TEMPURA

**SERVES 4**

8 large raw prawns, peeled and deveined

4 scallops, cleaned

8 squid rings

200 g/7 oz firm white fish fillets, cut into strips

150 g/5¹/₂ oz packet tempura mix

oil, for deep-frying

few drops of sesame oil

*To serve*

shoyu (Japanese soy sauce)

Make little cuts on the underside of the prawns to keep them straight while they cook. Pull any membranes off the squid rings.

Combine the tempura mix with the amount of water described on the packet instructions until you have a lumpy batter full of air bubbles. Do not try to make the batter smooth or it will be heavy, and make sure you use it straight away or it will settle.

Drop all the seafood into the batter.

Heat the oil in a deep-fryer to 180–190°C/ 350–375°F, or until a cube of bread browns in 30 seconds. Add a few drops of sesame oil to the fryer.

Add the tempura in batches of 2–3. If you add too many pieces at one time the oil temperature will drop and the batter will be soggy. When the tempura pieces are a very light golden colour, which should take only 2–3 minutes, take them out and try to drain off as much oil as possible. Leave them to drain on a piece of kitchen paper for 30 seconds to blot up more oil.

Serve this dish very hot with shoyu as a dipping sauce.

TEMPURA MIX IS AVAILABLE IN PACKETS AND JUST NEEDS TO BE MIXED WITH WATER. DON'T BE TEMPTED TO MAKE A SMOOTH BATTER BECAUSE A LUMPIER BATTER WORKS BETTER.

# MISO SOUP

**SERVES 4**

1 litre/1³/4 pints water

2 teaspoons powdered dashi

175 g/6 oz block soft tofu, cut into 1-cm/¹/2-inch cubes

4 shiitake or button mushrooms, sliced

4 tbsp miso

2 spring onions, chopped

Put the water and dashi in a saucepan and bring it to the boil. Add the tofu and mushrooms, turn down the heat and simmer gently for 3 minutes. Stir in the miso and simmer gently until it has dissolved completely. Turn off the heat, add the spring onion and serve straight away – the longer you leave miso the more it will settle and separate out.

DASHI IS A SOUP STOCK MADE FROM BONITO FLAKES, KOMBU AND WATER. IT IS AVAILABLE AS DASHI POWDER AND JUST NEEDS TO BE MIXED WITH WATER.

# INDEX